First published in Great Britain 1991
by Methuen Children's Books
Michelin House, 81 Fulham Road, London SW3 6RB
Illustrations copyright Librairie Hachette
All rights reserved
This presentation © 1991 Methuen Children's Books
Printed in Belgium by Proost

ISBN 0 416 17842 1

JEAN DE BRUNHOFF
BABAR'S
Baby Book
A record of the first five years

METHUEN CHILDREN'S BOOKS

The Birth

Name _____   Date _____

Time _____   Place _____

Doctor _____   Midwife _____

Weight _____

Length _____

Colour of eyes _____

Colour of hair _____

Announcement
(newspaper cutting or card)

The Family

Grandparents

_____

_____

_____

_____

Mother _____   Father _____

Brothers and Sisters

_____

_____

_____

Resemblances

Looks _____

_____

_____

Personality _____

_____

_____

Naming

Full Name _____

Date _____   Place _____

Guests _____

_____

_____

_____

Gifts _____

_____

_____

_____

Photographs

Progress

At one month

Weight _____

Length _____

At two months

Weight _____ Length _____

At three months

Weight _____ Length _____

At four months

Weight _____ Length _____

At five months

Weight _____ Length _____

At six months

Weight _____ Length _____

At seven months

Weight _____ Length _____

At eight months

Weight _____ Length _____

At nine months

Weight _____ Length _____

At ten months

Weight _____ Length _____

At eleven months

Weight _____ Length _____

At one year

Weight _____ Length _____

First Outings

Date   Place   To visit

_____ _____   _____

_____ _____   _____

_____ _____   _____

_____ _____   _____

Milestones

Smiles

___

Laughs

Stands

___

Sits

Walks

___

Crawls

Runs

Important Events

Ate first real food (date) _____

The food was _____

Was fully weaned (date) _____

Favourite food _____

_____

Important Events

Cut first teeth (date)

1 _____   5 _____   9 _____

2 _____   6 _____   10 _____

3 _____   7 _____   11 _____

4 _____   8 _____   12 _____

First had hair cut

Lock of hair

(date) _____

First Christmas

Spent at (place)

_____

Other people there

_____   _____

_____   _____

_____

Presents

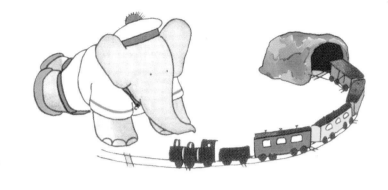

First Words

_____   _____

_____   _____

_____   _____

First Birthday

Spent at (place) _____

Party guests _____

_____

Presents _____

_____

_____

_____

_____

_____

Favourite Things

Favourite toys

_____

_____

_____

Favourite books

_____

_____

_____

Favourite games

_____

_____

_____

At two years

Height _____

Weight _____

Second birthday party

Party guests

Presents

_____

_____

_____

_____

_____

_____

_____

_____

Nursery School

Started on (date) _____

Name and address of school/playgroup

_____

_____

Special friends

_____ _____

Favourite activities

stories and songs   games and toys

_____ _____

_____ _____

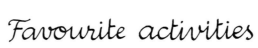

 # At three years

Height _____   Weight _____

Third birthday party

Party guests   Presents

_____   _____

_____   _____

_____   _____

_____   _____

At four years

Height _____   Weight _____

Fourth birthday party

Party guests   Presents

_____   _____

_____   _____

_____   _____

_____   _____

At five years

Height _____

Weight _____

Fifth birthday party

Party guests

Presents

_____

_____

_____

_____

_____

_____

_____

_____

First day at school

Date _____

Name and address of school

_____

_____

Teacher

_____

Favourite activities

_____

_____

_____

First writing & drawing